W9-BWR-610

QUIET PLACES

QUIET PLACES

How to create peaceful havens in your home, garden, and workplace

VINNY LEE

The Reader's Digest Association, Inc.
Pleasantville, NY / Montreal

QUIET PLACES

A **READER'S DIGEST SIMPLER LIFE**™ Book

Created and produced by Duncan Baird Publishers Limited

THE READER'S DIGEST ASSOCIATION, INC.
Executive Editor, Trade Books Joseph Gonzalez
Senior Design Director, Trade Books Henrietta Stern
Project Editor Deborah DeFord

DUNCAN BAIRD PUBLISHERS LIMITED
Managing Editor Catherine Bradley
Editor Maggie Ramsay
Designers Jeniffer Harte, Merideth Harte
Commissioned illustrations Jane Strother
Commissioned line artwork Peter Zangrillo
Picture research Nadine Bazar
Indexer Drusilla Calvert

The acknowledgments that appear on page 160 are hereby made a part of this copyright page.

Library of Congress Cataloging in Publication Data
Lee, Vinny.
Quiet Places: how to create peaceful havens in your home, garden, and workplace / Vinny Lee.
p. cm.
"A Reader's digest book."
Includes index.
ISBN 0-7621-0060-5
1. Interior decoration accessories. 2. Interior decoration--Psychological aspects. I. Title.
NK2115.5.A25L44 1998
747'.9—DC21 98-5092

Typeset in Transitional 521
Color reproduction by Colourscan, Singapore
Printed in the United States of America

Peace be to this house, and to all that dwell in it.

Book of Common Prayer

Contents

Achieving Serenity

Life often seems busy, noisy, and stressful. The calm of the natural world—as when a clear, azure sky is reflected in peaceful, unruffled waters—may seem far removed from the tumult of everyday concerns. Faced with many demands on our time and attention, we often begin to feel out of tune with nature, an experience described by the English poet William Wordsworth: "The world is too much with us; late and soon, / Getting and spending, we lay waste our powers; / Little we see in Nature that is ours." To counteract daily pressures and achieve true harmony in our lives, we need to regain an affinity with the natural world. We can set out on the path to inner serenity by creating a haven from intrusion, a quiet place where we can restore our energies.

Your haven may be a particular room or a favorite area, however small, within your home or garden; by adding a few simple touches you can make it a peaceful sanctuary. Begin by surrounding yourself with colors, textures, and scents that calm and please you. Choose shapes that are easy to live with, and keep colors harmonious so that the senses are soothed and refreshed, rather than overstimulated. Express your personal taste even further through art and mementoes, choosing elements carefully to evoke tranquility.

A keynote of simplicity will enhance a room's sense of space and serenity—but remember that simple does not mean spartan. Against a plain background, for example, a bowl of wild flowers or a wood-framed mirror becomes a focal point for the imagination. In a Japanese custom, decorative objects are stored in a chest beneath an alcove. Each item is, in turn, displayed alone in the alcove so that its singular beauty can be appreciated.

When creating your special place, turn to nature's colors, textures, and scents for decorating schemes, furniture, and finishing touches. "Forest" colors, for example, are the rich greens and browns of living trees and the dappled earth floor below. They are linked with the musky aroma of cedar and the revitalizing fragrance of pine, and they harmonize well with the fibrous textures of linen and cotton.

"Water," for lovers of the seashore and sky, is reflected in shades of blue, from pale and silvery to warmer turquoise. Associated textures include cool slate and velvety corduroy.

"Citrus" fruit colors—from vibrant orange to the softer shades of pale yellow and watered lime—are refreshing, and their scents cleanse and invigorate. Waffle-weave fabrics capture the spirit of youthful freshness and exhilaration.

"Floral" colors include the soft pinks, purples, crimsons, and reds that characterize fragrant blooms such as roses, violets, sweet peas, and lilies. The sensuous, petal-like textures of silk and satin complement this glamorous palette.

"Spice," heady and exotic, is evoked by shades of warm orange, gold, and tan-brown, and through scents of cinnamon, cloves, and anise. Its luxurious seductiveness is emphasized by richly textured fabrics such as tapestry, voile, and fine wool.

Use these themes to bring a calming sense of the natural world indoors. Even in the smallest city apartment you can create a link with nature by growing potted plants on a windowsill or planting colorful window boxes.

The Art of Repose

Every room or space has the potential to become a quiet place —a relaxing environment where you can unwind and seek serenity. You can create surroundings conducive to such tranquility by carefully mixing color and light, and by subtly combining texture, tone, and shape. Add evocative scents that calm the mind and, to enhance your oasis of peace further, create resting points for the eye: small cameo or still-life "pictures" that bring pleasure. These can be as simple as an elegant chair, a book, or a blossoming plant.

Secrets of Shape

The shape and size of any room may appear to be fixed features, but imaginative use of color and pattern can create very different impressions of even a small area. Shape is an important part of a room's individuality, and any unusual angles, alcoves, windows, and doorways should be exploited.

The imposing effect of high ceilings can be softened by painting them in dark, rich color tones, which may be echoed on the lower half of the walls. Paneling or faux painted panels also "shorten" a high wall to give a more welcoming effect. In a small room, keep the colors light to maximize the space. A white ceiling will "rise" rather than "press down," while the decorators' trick of creating a wide band of white around the top of the wall adds to the illusion of height.

Color and pattern also affect our perception of other dimensions. You can make a long, narrow room appear wider by using strong color on the far wall to bring it forward. Because the eye is drawn along lines, floorboards that are laid crosswise can accentuate the width of a narrow hallway.

Spaces Within Spaces

The main area of most rooms can be divided into a number of smaller spaces, each with their own character. These "inner sanctums" may be defined by existing features, such as a chimney breast, staircase, or sloping attic roof, or may be created, for example when you add a built-in bookshelf. A walk-in closet may become a room in itself, perhaps a home office or play area, balancing practical requirements with ingenuity and imagination.

Few rooms, even in the most modern apartment, contain only four flat walls. Most possess several recesses that can accommodate a chair or some bookshelves, a special picture or a favorite plant. A change of color tone highlights the shape; if the main walls are soft yellow, for example, a deeper shade in the recess will bring a feeling of depth and definition to the space.

Walls are also broken by doorways, offering a visual frame for spaces beyond the immediate area. If the door opens onto a garden or another room with a pleasant aspect, the door jamb and lintel can be accentuated like a picture frame to emphasize the attractive view.

The Spirit of Intimacy

Even within a large space, intimate areas can be created by arranging furniture in smaller, convivial groups. Such organization, which in effect produces several individual "rooms" within an open-plan framework, is particularly well suited to loft apartments and converted barn homes, characterized by spaces without conventional boundaries.

A sofa, for example, may be placed in the center of a room to form a barrier or low wall. It offers a demarcation between one half of a room and the other, and between functions such as dining and sitting. Two sofas facing each other will make a wide room feel less spacious, while a circle of chairs around a low table encourages an atmosphere of comfortable informality.

- Choose furnishings for their comfort. Traditional high-back, upholstered easy chairs with wings or enveloping arms cocoon the sitter securely. Scatter pillows and rolls offer additional support if needed.
- If you have stone or wooden floors, place a rug in the center of your cozy circle to introduce softness and warmth.

The Play of Light and Shade

Daylight is one of nature's greatest gifts: it warms and nurtures, and it creates constantly varying patterns of light and shadow. Differences in daylight's strength and direction can alter the mood of a room throughout the day and through the seasons, as light slips from brilliant and white to soft and golden. When positioning furniture, try to match its function to the light: set a breakfast table by a window that receives morning rays; place a desk or chair beneath a skylight to use afternoon sun for studying or sewing.

Sometimes natural light is insufficient. If so, consider which artificial light sources match your needs, and decide whether you want bright light to work by, a subtle glow for relaxing, or colored lightbulbs to enhance tones within a decorative scheme. Dimmer switches allow flexibility between low light for intimate moments and brighter light for reading. Different types of artificial light have marked effects on colors, so check samples of paint and fabrics in both natural and artificial light before choosing.

Directing Light

As natural light enters a room through doorways and windows, it is narrowed and directed from the start. It tends to fall in pools or shafts that follow the movement of the sun, highlighting the rhythms of the day and the seasons. You can mimic these aspects of nature's lighting in your selection of lamps and window treatments.

Allow window dressings to alter the direction and emphasis of natural light. Morning and summer light may cause glare that can be stressful and punishing on the eyes. Diffuse too-bright daylight with a voile drape or a muslin shade. The gentler light characteristic of the fall is attractive and relaxing, but it is difficult to work by unless it is well directed. Pull drapes to the edge of the window frame and tie them back to allow maximum light into the room.

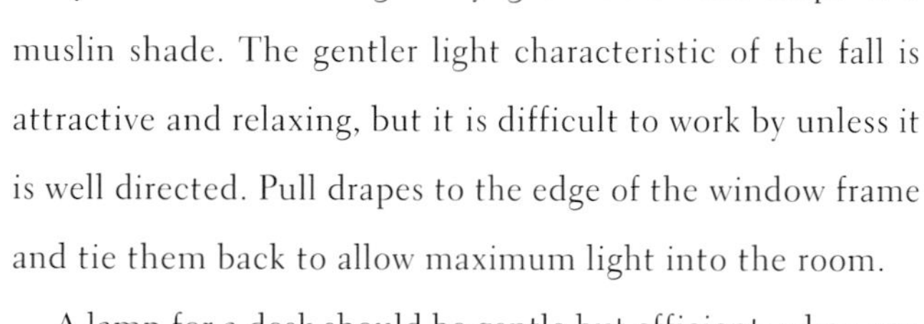

A lamp for a desk should be gentle but efficient; when you switch it off, try to turn on another light to give your eyes and thoughts a new focus. Indirect lighting creates pools of light on walls and ceilings to bathe a room in a soft glow.

• Adjust the slats of Venetian blinds to redirect shafts of light in accordance with your needs or moods.

• Softly tinted light encourages contemplation, and you don't need to fit stained glass to achieve the effect, as long as you have a well-lit door or window. Let light pass through a drape or shade in a translucent ink-blue fabric to create a reflective mood; rays that pass through a vermilion fabric will bring a comforting warmth.

Mirrors and Reflections

Mirrors have long had magical associations and are often referred to in fairy tales and legends, in which their role may be either innocent or wicked. An old, mottled looking glass seems to give a glimpse into another world, silent and mysterious, where nothing is quite what it seems. Two or more mirrors set at angles to each other produce a maze of reflected images and offer the chance to see ourselves, unexpectedly, from a new perspective. The skillful use of mirrors can create intriguing illusions of space, while serving as an attractive way to increase the light in a room.

A dark passageway, for example, can be brightened by positioning a large, preferably tall, mirror at its end. Even without natural light, the mirror will play back the glow of a lightbulb or the light from a doorway. If a room has only one small window, you will double its effectiveness by placing a large mirror at an appropriate angle to reflect the light into the room. Mirrors also act as windows by providing a bright reflection on a solid wall. A large, unframed wall mirror will appear to increase the space in a room by suggesting a further dimension.

• Place an object in front of a mirror to enjoy the beauty of a favorite piece of pottery or a vase of flowers from every angle.

• Group small, different-shaped mirrors together to produce a mosaic-like picture of reflections.

• Create a trompe l'oeil archway in your garden by framing a tall, narrow mirror with trelliswork or climbing plants.

Shadows and Shapes

All around us, indoors and out, subtly shifting patterns of light and shade provide a theater of continual change; we can find refreshment and calm by exploring the shadows as well as the light. In the natural world, the shade beneath a leafy tree is caressed by soft, dappled light. If sunlight is too bright or hot for comfort, we are drawn to the cool stillness of the contrasting deep shade. Our imagination fastens on shadows that sway in the breeze or lengthen as they move away from the light source.

Within the home, areas of shadow and light may be used to reflect different moods: the bright side of a room near a window may be either peaceful or stimulating, depending upon the time of the day or the season, whereas the shadowy inner part of the room, perhaps by the fireplace, will be most cozy and comforting in the winter.

In daylight or artificial light, an unusual ornament or piece of furniture, or a shaped screen, can be moved until it casts a pleasing shadow. Alternatively, choose your own shadow pattern with a simple pierced-tin lantern.

Plants create a pleasing silent shadow play with every passing movement. The flickering light from oil lamps or candles—in a wall sconce or candlestick, or floating in a dish of water—casts dancing shadows that are enchanting and entertaining to watch. Despite their beauty, remember never to leave burning candles unattended.

Patterns of Calm

Nature has designed a spectacular variety of patterns to soothe and delight us: the bark and branches of trees, the stars in the night sky, rippled sands, the marbled symmetry of a butterfly's wings, the elaborate lace of a spider's web. Such patterns have, throughout the course of civilization, inspired much of the human design we encounter in architecture and interior design. In creating our personal sanctuaries, we may refer to nature's patterns for the associations they bring or for the calming influence of their repetitive rhythms.

Wooden paneling and floorboards, for example, form a regular pattern of narrow strips, but within each board the grain of the wood has its own unique design, following the knots and growth rings of the tree. Tiles, especially in natural terracotta, handmade ceramic, or quarried stone, may show individual variations in color and texture, but the overall effect will be of their repeating geometric outlines. These natural patterns can easily be mixed without disturbing the harmony of a room.

Simple Stencils

Simple decoration is the easiest way to achieve a calm environment, but a complete absence of pattern can be rather austere. A stencil offers a unique embellishment to highlight certain areas of the room—within an alcove, for example, or around the top of a wall or a doorway. Stenciling allows you to control the amount and strength of design in the room and, if you wish, to choose a motif that recurs on fabric, furniture, and even stationery.

To make a stencil, decide on a feature with a distinctive outline, such as an oak leaf, a stylized flower head with curling tendrils, a horizontal "S" that can be linked to form a chain, or maybe a design of personal significance. The pattern should be drawn on a piece of heavy cardboard and cut out to form a template through which paint can be applied. The template can be flipped to make the pattern appear at reverse angles.

• Vary the size or color of your chosen motif. For example, two or three shades of green could be used with the same leaf template; a shell could be stenciled large on bathroom paneling, small on a towel.

• Paint can be easily applied through a stencil with a sponge or large bristle brush. Dab the paint through the shape, rather than brushing it solidly, to achieve a softer, more harmonious effect.

• Use fabric paints and pens to decorate material. The design may also need to be set by pressing it with a warm iron.

Thought Patterns

Sometimes we can effectively calm the mind by focusing on something other than our busy thoughts. Pattern may be a catalyst in this relaxation process. A design that is familiar or one that requires concentration can draw the imagination away from worries and problems, facts and figures, toward a state of tranquility. In a plain setting, pattern can be introduced in the form of a framed print or wall hanging, as a mosaic, on pottery, or as a rug, throw, or pillow.

Among the oldest patterns still found today are those from African, Aboriginal, or Native North American cultures. Many are geometric, stylized shapes that are symbolic of landscapes, animals, and stars. More recent forms of traditional design, such as those seen on Amish quilts, have their own compelling symmetry and can provide a reassuring link with our past.

Mandalas—symbols of the universe and spiritual progress—are used as an aid to Buddhist and Hindu meditation. Reflecting on their designs can bring a sense of peace and harmony, even if we do not follow these religions.

Patterns on Fabric

Fabric with an overall design or a border motif provides a focal point that can determine the way we perceive a room. Whether the fabric is used to cover furniture, floor, walls, or windows, it will introduce warmth, color, and a welcoming mood. The scale of the design should reflect the size of the room. If a stripe or floral motif is too large, it will be overpowering, while too small a pattern may appear weak or insignificant. Complex needlework, such as a patchwork quilt or embroidered wall hanging, is best displayed against a plain setting so that the pattern can be appreciated. Create a delicate balance of plain and pattern by introducing the latter a little at a time and repeating similar patterns across the room. Checks and stripes, for example, have a common geometric theme. Leaf motifs blend happily with florals if the basic shapes are harmonious: sinuous and elegant or gently rounded. Diverse patterns can be linked if they feature the same family of color tones.

Texture provides a key element of fabric pattern as well—the interlocking "V"s of a herringbone weave, for example, or the speckled mélange of tweed.

Harmonious Textures

The juxtaposition of hard and soft textures can bring a variety of moods to a room. For example, by covering a wall with planks of wood, you evoke the relaxed, informal atmosphere of a country lodge or mountain hut. If the wood is planed and varnished, or used as paneling, it gives the room a greater feeling of serenity or of a refined period style. Smooth plaster, exposed or painted brick walls, or slate used as flooring or work surfaces, gives the uncluttered elegance of urban chic. Some people find this simplicity soothing in itself, while others prefer to soften the hard edges with rugs of sumptuous silk or thick wool. The rugs seem even more luxurious in contrast to the plain background.

Window treatments can also use textures to create tranquil effects. For example, fine voile curtains set behind thick drapes will appear delicate and halo-like around the edge of the outer fabric. If hung the other way around, the outer layer of voile will bring a softening influence to both the weight and the color of the heavier fabric.

Walls of Character

A single color on the walls can establish the overall mood of your quiet place, but a decorative paint treatment such as sponging or graining refines the effect. In a new apartment, simple techniques add character, texture, and depth to a fresh, smooth surface. Older walls respond well to paint treatments that disguise minor blemishes and make a feature of their time-worn appearance. Many effects can be created inexpensively with everyday materials such as a sponge, a rolled rag, or a hard bristle brush.

Color washing with a large brush results in gentle undulations of watery color and creates a mood of rustic charm. Sponging gives a mottled effect; depending on the colors chosen it can be soft and subtle or may achieve definite areas of contrast. Dipping a crumpled rag into paint, then rolling it over the wall achieves longer, more jagged lines of color; the type of cloth determines whether the lines are hard or soft.

Combing or graining surfaces with a special tool imitates the natural grace of wood. More complex faux finishes may simulate the cool elegance of marble and granite.

• You will need to dilute the paint for a subtly blended effect, but do this with care, as a solution that is too watery will form rivulets.

• Practice your chosen technique first on a sheet of paper so that you can gauge the strength of color, thickness of paint, and overall effect.

• Do not press the sponge or material to the wall with too much force. The best effects are achieved with a dab or roll that is gentle as a kiss.

Natural Fabrics

Natural materials are resilient and charming, with a feel that few artificial fabrics can imitate successfully. Most natural fabrics withstand regular wear—in fact they may become more attractive with years of use. Cloth made from natural fibers tends to have a soft drape and even when wrinkled and worn can impart an impression of quality.

Linen, cotton, and wool can be woven or knitted into many different textures, from rough and rugged to gossamer-fine and floaty. They can be brushed to make them warm and snug or polished to give them a smart sheen; they may retain their natural color or be dyed to complement their setting, but their inherent qualities remain in any variation. These fabrics bring us into harmony with nature and can suggest warmth in winter and coolness in summer.

Natural materials need not be made into cloth for us to appreciate their calming properties. Hemp, jute, willow, wicker, and seagrass bring their own sense of serenity to furniture, floor coverings, and finishing touches.

Touches of Luxury

For sensual indulgence and relaxation, your haven may contain items chosen purely for the opulence or delicacy of their textures. These luxuries may change with the seasons or your moods, but remember that a little richness can go a long way—be selective and choose a few favorite pieces rather than accumulating clutter. Glamour does not preclude practicality: in a bathroom, thick, fluffy towels are the height of luxury. In a bedroom, fresh linen or cotton sheets are the ultimate indulgence in the heat of summer, while in winter a soft wool blanket or a cashmere throw is warm and comforting.

Velvety and silky textures are found in the natural world in the coats of animals, birds' plumage, and flower petals. In the home these textures can be echoed in jewel-colored velvet drapes, silk throws and table coverings, and creamy smooth satin pillows. Sumptuous brocade, intricate embroidery, and delicate lace evoke times gone by or exotic countries you may dream of visiting. Use these fabrics in small, elegant touches to conjure up your own sense of tranquility and peace.

Colors of Nature

Nature's palette is based on the browns, greens, blues, and grays of earth and forest, sky and water. Snow, clouds, and blossoms on trees add highlights. While extremely varied, this range of colors is essentially restful and can be used in any room to suggest harmony with nature. At the same time, the natural world displays surprisingly vivid colors: a rainbow, the fleeting fires of sunset, exotic birds, fish in a coral reef, wild flowers, and trees in the fall. From this extensive palette we can devise our own pleasing combinations to establish a personal sense of quiet.

White and cream create a pristine and serene environment and encourage calm feelings. Against a pale background you can add "gems" of color—plants, pictures, pieces of furniture, rugs—that blend or contrast.

Wood brings a sense of natural life to any setting. Its colors range from pale sun-bleached driftwood and elegant beech, through golden pine and deep red cherrywood, to time-darkened oak and ebony. Wicker furniture and hemp floor coverings provide textural contrasts in natural browns.

Colors of the Earth

Earth colors, drawn from rocks and soils, convey a feeling of endurance and solidity. The palette tends to be muted and subtle, varying in hue from the cool whites, grays, and pinks of marble, slate, and granite, through the yellow tones of desert sands, to the warmer rusts and deep red-brown shades of monumental rocks.

In warmer climates, terracotta and ocher pigments are used in washes on both exterior and interior walls; such effects are often mimicked indoors in colder countries to suggest the sensation of the sun's heat and vitality. Earth tones have a wise, dependable aspect, acknowledged in Robert Browning's poem "Among the Rocks": "Oh, good gigantic smile o' the brown old earth…Such is life's trial, as old earth smiles and knows."

- Bring the reassuring colors of the earth into the kitchen or dining room by using rustic glazed terracotta plates for a variety of foods.
- Use slate table mats to provide cool, natural focal points.

Colors of Sky and Water

Blue tones, including turquoise and light gray, are restful, spiritual colors with the power to still the mind. Often linked with meditation, these hues draw upon associations with the sea's waves and continually changing sky to suggest fluidity and a cleansing of mind and body. Color therapists have shown that the contemplation of blue can lower blood pressure and relieve insomnia, making it the perfect choice for an office or bedroom. In a child's room, blue combines its freshness and its soothing qualities to bring an enveloping sense of peace. Blues are sometimes felt to be cold colors, but this need not be the case—think of an azure summer sky or warm, inviting, tropical waters. Pale blues are gentle and graceful, but deeper blues are best used sparingly in a room, for example on a pillow or as drapes.

- Add a touch of natural blue with flowers. Shades vary from pale to deep, seen in bluebonnets, bachelor's buttons, and delphiniums.
- Hang landscapes and seascapes to bring the blues of the sky and the ocean into windowless areas.

Colors of Forest and Garden

When thinking of quiet places, many of us imagine a mossy bank by a river, a peaceful, flower-filled garden, or a field of long grass swaying in a breeze. These reveries share a common fascination with plant life and its associated color, green. This hue is linked with harmony and rejuvenation, which are often the beneficial results of a period of calm reflection. Green's varied tones reflect the changing seasons of the year, from the vibrant freshness of spring growth to the darker, glossy evergreens of winter.

As the Irish ballad claims, there are at least "forty shades of green," from acidic lime to silvery moss, from fresh apple to subtle olive and blue-green pine, each of which conjures up individual pictures and scents. Over large areas, the paler shades can create an elegant effect; darker tones, often combined with wood paneling, suggest the comfortable seclusion of the club or the meditative quiet of a library. Very bright greens are best confined to a single wall or window area, since they can be overstimulating. Green can also be introduced in small touches as paintwork, pillows, or indoor plants.

Indoor Green

Houseplants introduce living color to any environment. The attraction of watching their color subtly change as each plant develops will encourage peaceful thoughts, and caring for plants will bring its own rewards when you see new shoots or leaves unfurling. Seasonal plants such as spring bulbs—hyacinths, narcissi, and tulips—can be "forced" to bloom early indoors, heralding the new season's mood, colors, and scents. For a simple green highlight, choose a single plant that has pleasing foliage; for a harmonious patchwork of different greens, with the added interest of intriguing textures and shapes, plan an architectural grouping for a table or your desk at work.

Offices are often air-conditioned and dry, which does not suit all plants, but it is not difficult to create a small oasis or leafy screen on or near your desk. Cacti and other succulents thrive in a dry environment; their shapes are fascinating, and when they bloom the colors are brilliant. Cacti can be grouped together in a bowl, their soil topped with gravel to retain moisture. Do not overwater them—just think of their home, the desert. They won't suffer when you are away on vacation.

Complements to Greenery

To achieve the most peaceful effect from indoor plants, try to link the room's color scheme to green. Yellows and blues provide harmonious backdrops, since these two colors combine to form the many shades of green, each with their own impact: blue-greens tend to be calming, yellow-greens more refreshing. Warmer yellows suggest sunlight and optimism, which can be emphasized by the addition of plants. White and cream are also compatible with green and provide a serene setting for plants. Avoid opposite color—such as red or strong orange—which can be unsettling to the eye.

Although houseplants suit most sites and situations, some are more appropriate to certain colors and rooms than to others. For example, in a dark room, heavy, shady plants will be lost in the general scheme. Instead, use the dark background to emphasize the delicacy of lighter green varieties with fern-like or frond-like leaves. Many plants enjoy the steam and warmth of a bathroom. Ferns, glossy-leaved plants, and certain orchids thrive in these surroundings. You can add a fresh look with daisy-like marguerites.

Touches of Color

A calm environment will be based on tones from nature's core palette, but to bring a room to life requires touches of brilliant color, mirroring the glorious hues of the flowers and birds that animate the natural world.

A vase of freshly cut flowers or a bowl of spring bulbs add temporary splashes of vivacity to a room. Bright pillows on a sofa, an area rug, a painting, or a piece of sculpture against a plain wall, can be changed occasionally, perhaps to reflect the seasons. As a more permanent feature, colored glass inset in a door or window, whether it fills the pane or forms a jewel-like border, comes to life when light shines through it. The light, endowed with color, then creates a vibrant, shifting mosaic on a floor, wall, or other surface.

- Place crystal prisms on a sunny window ledge to cause tiny rainbows to appear on walls.
- Fix a glass shelf in front of a window to provide a display area for colored bottles that glow when sunlight is behind them.

THE VENETO

Moods of Color

Color, whether gentle hues from nature's palettes or bright modern shades, can dramatically affect how people feel. Light, fresh tones are generally refreshing and soothing, while darker colors envelop, comfort, and protect; yet response to color tends to be very personal and cannot be prescribed. Some people find blue restful and calming, others consider it too cool; to one person, orange is hot and overstimulating, while someone else relishes the warmth that the color emits. The key is to find a color with which you feel at peace and then work with it as a base or use it as a theme, setting tranquil touches of color against a serene background.

Dark or muted colors can create a feeling of contemplative calm or quiet elegance. For example, a traditional study, lined with bookcases of leather-bound volumes, is often decorated in deep green, red, or blue. These colors work well in artificial light, typically the main source of illumination. Rich red wine colors, used for chair covers, candles, or napkins, bring a relaxing air of luxury to a dining room.

• Avoid stark contrasts by choosing shades that complement each other. For example, burgundy upholstery may make white walls look bare and cold, but adding cream or a hint of pink to walls will provide a little warmth and work well with the rich color of the fabric.

Sources of Scent

Scents often evoke particular times and places, and these memories can be calming and enjoyable. Vanilla is said to have a "motherly" smell that is reassuring and comforting. The gentle fragrance of rose may be similarly soothing—although to others it is also sensual and erotic. Lavender and jasmine can be at the same time relaxing and reviving.

In the language of the perfumer, scents fall into six main family groups—floral, woody, spicy, resinous, citrus, and herbaceous—that can be combined in certain proportions to create an agreeable blend. When introducing fragrance into your home, whether through potpourri, room sprays, or fresh or dried flowers, analyze the type and proportion of the scents, and try to visualize the colors of the perfumes; if they create a harmonious palette they will, more often than not, sit happily together. If making a potpourri for a bedroom, for example, try mixing the subtle floral scent of rose petals with the less sweet and more herbal fragrance of lavender, for a soothing blend to ease away the stress of the day.

Fragrance for the Home

There are many ways in which fragrance can transform the atmosphere of our home or workplace. Aromatic candles and room sprays allow us to match our mood with the freshness of citrus, the invigoration of the seashore, or any number of evocative floral scents. Many products draw on the principles of aromatherapy: the use of essential oils extracted from plants to relieve both physical and mental ailments, or, more generally, to relax or revitalize. For a fragrance to remain with us all day, we can add a few drops of essential oil to the bathwater or dilute them in a carrier oil (almond or grapeseed) for a body massage. In the home, essential oils can be used in a burner to create a romantic, uplifting, or soothing atmosphere, according to the oil used.

There is nothing, however, quite like fresh or dried plants to provide a feast for all the senses. Bunches of herbs in the kitchen, a garland of lavender for the bedroom, or a vase of old-fashioned scented roses in the living room offer pleasing colors, shapes, and textures to complement their scents.

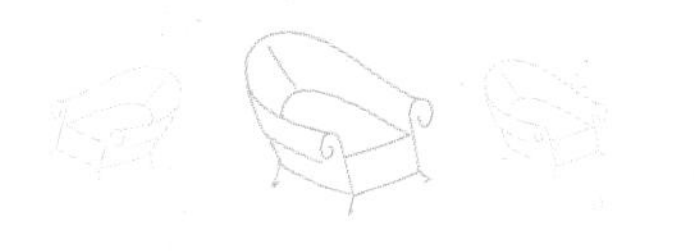

Restful Rooms

Your haven of quiet should be part of your everyday surroundings, ready to restore your sense of peace at any moment. Any room in your home can be decorated and furnished in a way that will help you find your ease there, and part of your workplace can be designated as a personal oasis of calm. Avoiding clutter is a main requirement, as is a comfortable ambient temperature. Whatever the room, you can enhance feelings of tranquility by carefully choosing fabrics, shapes, and calming colors, and by adjusting the lighting and fragrance to suit your mood.

The Heart of the Home

The main room of any home, the living room, is often a hub of social activity. However, with a harmonious color scheme, comfortable furniture, and versatile lighting, the living room can also be a peaceful haven in which you can relax with friends or family, listen to soothing music, enjoy an engrossing hobby, or retreat into the world of a good book.

Traditionally, the focal point of a living room is the hearth, with its associations of warmth and security. If you are lucky enough to have a real fire, the flickering flames bring the room to life in winter; in summer the fireplace can be filled with the colors, shapes, and textures of a houseplant, or a vase of dried or fresh flowers.

If you don't have a hearth, try to create an alternative focal point. It might be a shelf, small chest, or table upon which you can display favorite ornaments, photographs, flowers, candlesticks, and a clock. Dancing candle flames and the ticking of a clock have a reassuring quality similar to that provided by a fire.

Sitting in Serenity

Comfortable seating is essential to a relaxing environment, and the color, pattern, and texture of soft accents can subtly determine the atmosphere of any living room. Relatively inexpensive and easy to change, they are among the most flexible and personal ingredients of a particular space. Pillows, for example, are available in many shapes and sizes, from small Oriental neck rolls to modern triangles and the traditional, much-loved square. Choose a form of pillow to complement the setting, perhaps to emphasize a feature, such as a round window or diamond panes of glass, or to add interest and vitality to a plain sofa through a mixture of shapes and colors. Be imaginative as well in your choice of fabrics. Combine smooth and textured fabrics on different sides of the same pillow for a quick and easy decorative change. Trimmings may also be selected from a wide range of textures, either accentuating or contrasting with the pillow material.

Sofa throws, shaped like a shawl or small blanket and made from lightweight cotton or heavier woollen tweed, bring cozy homeliness to angular sofas or armchairs and introduce a new focus to the decorative scheme.

• Transform your old pillows with new finishes. Use imaginative trimmings to highlight the pillows' shapes and to harmonize with their colors and patterns. Choose a plain trim, matching piping, or an elaborate tie made with contrasting ribbon or rope.

• Introduce double-sided sofa throws to vary the room's mood, with everyday material on one side and more luxurious fabric on the other.

Design for Living

Many of the most harmonious living spaces combine soft, rounded shapes with crisper, more angular styles of design. Pointed corners and straight lines may seem to "cut" aggressively into the space around them, making them less immediately soothing. Yet the clean, graphic effect they create can be calming if not used to excess.

The secret lies in balancing the shapes of a room's features and furnishings to achieve a serene, complementary pattern. Consider how individual items of furniture will harmonize with the room's main features. If you place an armchair with rounded back and arms in front of a tall, oblong window, you will lessen the impact of the structure's parallel lines and create an agreeable arrangement. To emphasize the height and shape of the window, on the other hand, place an upright dining chair with a fine, linear frame close beside it to echo the shape and double the visual impact.

• Soften the harsh edges of a table with the gentle folds of a cloth. If you do not wish to cover the whole table, place

a narrow runner of cloth in the table's center and allow it to tumble over the edges at opposite sides.

• If you have too many soft, round armchairs, introduce square pillows for a contrasting, angular note. Flexible, down-filled pillows will make a deep sofa feel less engulfing and provide useful back or arm support.

• The parallel lines formed by rows of shelves can be made less severe by adding trailing pot plants that grow down and partially cover them.

Rooms for the Mind

The type of environment in which you work best depends on you, although usually only home workers possess the flexibility to explore their preferences fully. A well-planned workplace can make use of a relatively small area in the house—perhaps a walk-in closet or the unused space tucked under the stairs. A few guidelines will help you to develop a compact, attractive, and efficient home office, encouraging concentration and minimizing wasted time.

- Good lighting is important: if daylight is accessible, position your workstation to take best advantage of it. Supplement daylight with an adjustable tasklamp that can be directed onto your work.
- Use space creatively; if you sometimes need a large surface, try a pair of trestle supports and a large board or piece of wood that can be assembled when required, then dismantled.
- Keep the floorspace clear, and have reference books close at hand.

INDIA
HIMALAYAN ART

An Oasis of Calm

Many people work under difficult conditions in which serenity seems hard to achieve, yet sound principles of design and a few small, personal items can transform the office into an agreeable and harmonious setting.

To make the working day less physically stressful, ensure that your desk or workstation is at a comfortable height and the chair correctly adjusted to provide good lower back support (bring in extra soft pillows if necessary). Remember to take regular breaks, walking around to stretch and exercise your body, as well as resting your eyes from a screen or other close work.

Use natural light as much as possible, and try to remain aware of the outside world during your day—look through a window occasionally, or keep seasonal flowers, fruit, or potpourri nearby.

- Add personal touches to your work area to make it a friendlier, more relaxing place. These may include pots of cuttings from a plant at home, photographs of friends or family, collectibles, candies, or assorted memorabilia.

• Change these items regularly, perhaps using a seasonal theme or following anniversaries, to ensure that you continue to notice and appreciate them. Avoid the temptation to clutter your desk with too many mementoes—quality is more important than quantity!

The Quiet Kitchen

Around mealtimes the kitchen is usually a hive of industry, but at other periods of the day it can be a refuge, filled with the comforting aromas of freshly made coffee or bread baking in the oven. The decorative scheme can help to establish a mood of serenity: while a kitchen needs to be easy to clean, with clear lighting over work surfaces, its functional elements can be kept soft and harmonious. A subtle wall color, such as primrose yellow or pale violet-blue, can feel fresh and cheerful in the morning or daylight, yet warm and welcoming in the evening or artificial light. Patterned shades or curtains, and a vase of flowers, add vivid splashes of color. Seat pads can be added to hard kitchen chairs to make the environment more restful.

Achieving a calm kitchen calls for a certain amount of organization—clutter and disorder cause feelings of unease. Just one clear countertop can create a sense of space, and there is immense satisfaction to be gained from seeing a kitchen, once filled with messy pans and bowls, transformed into a tidy room in which you can relax.

Starting Over

A relaxed start to the day is too important and enjoyable to be reserved for vacations and weekends. Calm, orderly beginnings enable both mind and body to recover from sleep and gently to adjust to the demands of the morning ahead. Even a few precious moments to linger over coffee, watch the sunlight stealing across the garden, indulge in a refreshing breakfast, and leaf through the newspaper in peace will significantly influence your mood and the general progress of the day to come.

Most people both prepare and eat breakfast in the kitchen, a room that plays an important part in achieving a harmonious beginning. It should have a feeling of spaciousness, which can be created through the design and layout of the room, with plenty of storage and a general lack of clutter. An attractive, functional, and organized room can be made even more conducive to a calm start by playing classical music or a recording of birdsong or waves falling on the seashore—often sold as relaxation tapes.

Pleasures of the Table

These days many of us eat "on the run," grabbing a snack from the refrigerator, then dashing on to the next business, social, or sporting activity. The pleasure of sitting around a table to enjoy a meal is fast disappearing. Many apartments no longer have separate dining rooms; the area set aside for eating may be part of the kitchen or living room. This makes it even more important to achieve a relaxed and stress-free environment for mealtimes.

Traditional dining rooms often include red in their color scheme. Essentially warm and welcoming, darker wine-reds are more elegant, orange tones more cheerful and sociable. Plain or simply-decorated cloths and plates in whites, creams, and solids provide the best setting for food; highly patterned tableware may be fun, but it can confuse and distract the eyes.

Daylight brings its own natural calm. Artificial lighting should be directed away from diners' eyes, while allowing them to appreciate the food on their plates. Candles help to create a mood of cozy intimacy; but make sure they offer sufficient light for a bright, rather than somber, atmosphere.

Setting the Mood

Setting a table is like designing theatrical scenery, in which the background makes an important contribution to the event's success. In some Asian countries there is a tradition known as "table talk"—rather than using matching plates and glasses, each setting reflects the interests of the person who is to sit there. For example, a keen gardener may have a green plate and a floral napkin tied with raffia, while a photographer may have a black napkin and a white plate. A table can be set to echo the theme of the food, for example with terracotta plates for Italian dishes, bistro-style gingham napkins for lunch with a French flavor, or rice bowls and chopsticks for a Chinese feast. A large, colorful, modern salad bowl would be in harmony with the spirit of a relaxing family lunch, while an antique tureen or crystal glasses would set the mood for a more formal meal.

Flowers for a dining table need not always be in a vase. At a romantic dinner, scatter rose petals across the cloth. For a summer lunch, tie the napkins with chives, tucking in a chive flower.

Gateways to Sleep

The bedroom should be the most restful room of all. Here, we need to unwind, settle the mind, and relax the body so that sleep will ensue. A comfortable bed, subtle lighting, and calm colors will all contribute to feelings of tranquility. A bedroom is also where the day begins, however, so the same environment must provide the stimulus to get up and get going. Keep the pathway to the door clear of clutter, and use simple variations to reflect the seasons. In summer a white or blue color scheme is cool and serene; for winter you might add a warm orange throw, or a soft rug to step on as you get in and out of bed. Darker walls can suggest luxury, but may feel stifling in warm weather. Emphasize the movement of air with fine voile drapes.

The bedroom is probably the most individual of home spaces. Small children draw comfort and security from mobiles and familiar toys as they drift toward sleep; teenagers can use this room to express their developing independence. Relatively bare, simple rooms are ideal "dream" rooms for some adults, while others prefer to rest their eyes on treasured possessions.

Indulging the Senses

Scent adds a touch of luxury, creating a mood of sensual relaxation and comfort. Certain aromas can have a positive influence on your state of mind; they may be evocative, soothing, or even sleep-inducing. For example, hops are widely believed to be calming, and lavender and rose inspire peaceful thoughts. Linen or muslin sachets can be filled with dried hop cones, lavender, or rose petals and hung on the bedpost near your head, tucked beneath a pillow, or left in a bowl on a mantelpiece or table. Bunches of lavender stems can also be grouped together and tied with ribbon or arranged in florists' foam to make a fragrant, attractive, and long-lasting bouquet.

A warm bath taken just before you go to bed allows you to gain maximum benefit from aromatic bath products. Encourage sweet dreams by adding a few drops of vanilla or almond essence to the water.

• Bring exotic, spicy, and citrus aromas to your closet or dressing table with a decorative pomander: an orange or lemon studded with whole

cloves. Push the cloves into the citrus peel in regular rows or at random, until the fruit is covered, then tie with a ribbon.

• Enhance a spicy potpourri with the interesting shapes and scents of nutmegs or cinnamon sticks—if you wish, tie the cinnamon sticks in bundles with silky ribbons.

The Delights of Dressing

Dressing can be a pleasure if, instead of racing against the clock or searching for missing items, we take time to enjoy the art of putting together an outfit in an orderly, well-lit space. In an ideal world we would all have a dressing room with ample storage, but this is rarely the case. To create a dressing area within your bedroom, you need little more than a chair or chest on which to lay out clothes, together with a mirror, preferably full length and near a source of natural light, to allow you to check your appearance before leaving the room. If carefully positioned, the mirror can also effectively increase the light in this area, making it bright and welcoming. A lightweight screen provides extra space for draping scarves or ties, and it can also serve as a partition that defines your dressing area.

You may need a window treatment that preserves your modesty while allowing access to as much natural light as possible. An unlined white drape or muslin shade will obscure the view but still let light through. Frosted glass in the lower part of the window has a similar, but more permanent, effect.

Bathroom Balm

The bathroom should be an intimate haven where you can enjoy solitude, whether it is for a few precious moments between waking and dressing, or for an indulgent soak in a bath scented with stress-relieving aromatic oils at the end of the day. Ideally, the bathroom provides a chameleon environment that can respond to these different needs. Lighting must be carefully planned for practical purposes, yet be subtle enough to relax by. Certain materials have a natural affinity with the bathroom setting: cork and wood—sealed against damp—to cover walls or floors, cotton toweling for draperies and mats. Calm colors and an uncluttered background allow you to add personal touches to define your individual sense of peace.

Shells make an appropriate decoration, evoking the cleansing water and invigorating air of the seashore. Thread them onto string for a vertical accent, or arrange them on a window ledge, perhaps with pieces of driftwood, sponges, or coral. Bottles of fragrant bath products suggest another source of pleasure and serenity.

Shapes and the Senses

Shapes are important in a bathroom because this is where the body is most vulnerable: you should be able to move freely without bumping against cold, hard, or rough surfaces or sharp edges. The bathroom is often the smallest room in a home, but you can maximize available space by retaining a keynote of simplicity and by distinguishing work-oriented areas from the restful accents within the room. Lightweight, movable screens are ideal for creating zones of peace and privacy. A screen can be folded flat and placed against the wall when not in use, or set up in another part of the room to give a different emphasis of shape and space.

Pedestal handbasins may sound a note of discord in the shape of the room. A practical solution is to set the basin into paneling or, if space permits, a cupboard. This finishes the room with a neat edge and provides useful storage: paneling forms a slim vanity unit for soaps, bottles, and brushes, or for a display of shells or natural sponges. On the other hand, a pedestal can introduce a graceful element and open up floor space.

Secrets of the Shower

A shower can be both stimulating and relaxing. The steady flow of water over the body does more than a simple cleansing; it also allows your mind a few minutes of peace. At the end of a stressful day a shower can seem to wash your troubles away, leaving you feeling refreshed and ready to face the world. Scent your skin with a luxurious soap or shower gel, using a soft sponge to maximize the gentle foam. For a truly indulgent experience, light fragrant candles whose aromas will linger in the warm, moist air.

The shower room's practical, hard surfaces can be softened with muted colors, rounded edging, and draped towels, all of which help to create a restful mood. An occasional patterned or stenciled tile provides a focal point as you wash. Cotton or cork mats offer a warm and welcoming place to stand when you step out of the shower. Stacks of thick, comforting toweling or soft waffle-weave linen or cotton towels make an attractive feature on a shelf or in a closet, as well as a gentle and pleasurable way to dry a freshly showered body. Many plants thrive in a humid atmosphere, and their natural shapes divert the eye from the hard edges of the shower enclosure.

The Garden Haven

Whether you seek sanctuary in a pocket-size patch of green in the concrete jungle of a city, or in a flower-filled bower in the country, to be in contact with plants and open air is deeply soothing. In these lines from a poem by the English poet Dorothy Gurney, the calming, spiritual effect of the garden is evoked: "The kiss of the sun for pardon, / The song of the birds for mirth, / One is nearer God's heart in a garden / Than anywhere else on earth." As the seasons pass, the intensity of light, colors, and foliage change, inspiring different moods of quiet: reviving, relaxing, or meditative.

One Step Beyond

Admiring a view from a window can be pleasant and calming, but to experience the sights, sounds, and scents of the natural world fully, we have to venture out of doors. A porch or veranda, suspended between house and garden, brings us closer to nature while offering shelter from the elements. Here, we can observe the movement of the seasons in comfort: the burst of new growth that follows springtime showers, the somnolent lushness of summer, the glorious, red-gold tapestry of leaves in the fall, frost glinting in the winter sunshine. Under protection of the house, the porch is an ideal place for babies to sleep or the elderly or convalescent to gain the benefit of fresh air. In warm weather a porch can also serve as an extra room in which to entertain friends, or simply to relax and read.

The gentle quality of natural light and shade can be felt most directly on the porch, making it a delightful place to enjoy periods of quiet contemplation. As daylight fades, lighting may be "borrowed" through the window of an inner room or chosen to reflect the colors of other outdoor lighting.

Relaxing on the Threshold

As you step into your garden, you enter space that is both a private sanctuary and part of the great outdoors. Without a ceiling overhead, you gain a refreshing awareness of a wider world, even from a small balcony, patio, or roof terrace. These are ideal areas to enjoy serene outdoor living and are most effective when simply furnished, with containers to create a particular mood or to complement other garden features. If you are able to alter the flooring, consider the different impact of a solid patchwork of weathered flagstone, or of bricks or tiles laid in straight or curving patterns.

- Position garden furniture carefully to take full advantage of natural light and garden views. A stone or brick plinth topped with wooden slats can serve as a bench or a table. In summer, you may wish to soften surfaces with foam pads and pillows.
- Sawn tree-trunks make charmingly natural outdoor furniture. A moderate-size trunk could provide a solid base for a table; an elegant larger one might be shaped to form a relaxing chair.

A Change of Pace

A garden can encourage relaxation by reminding us of the pattern of the seasons. As we move into the outdoor environment, our artificial perspectives and self-imposed deadlines are soothed by a recognition of nature's inexorable cycles. An awareness of seasonal change allows us to appreciate the diversity of the garden's moods and enjoy a steady succession of flowers, fruit, and foliage. It also enables us to plan a series of pleasant and well-ordered garden tasks, rather than a frantic annual cleanup!

Areas where sunlight readily promotes growth can be planted for changing displays of color and foliage. In spring, the intense purples and yellows of crocuses rise above the soil like small spears; daffodils and narcissi dance in the breeze and provide flowers for cutting. Summer brings a wider choice of sweet-smelling blooms to decorate the home. Fruit trees require most attention in the fall: their harvest needs to be made into pies or preserves; damaged fruit must be cleared before it rots. Plant evergreen shrubs for the dramatic winter appearance of their gem-like berries against glossy foliage.

The Garden Stroll

Within any garden there may be several areas of interest. Flowerbeds featuring one sole color of blooms complement others with strikingly shaped or patterned foliage, and delicate ground cover is offset by dense shrubs. Walking through a garden, however small, provides a sensual experience that reflects the time of day and the season. It also offers a valuable way to quiet troubled thoughts by focusing on the creativity of the natural world.

The path itself should add to the pleasure of the journey. Its particular surface—perhaps crunchy, colored gravel or rounded pebbles reminiscent of the seashore, bricks laid in a box or herringbone pattern, or softly yielding bark flakes—can help to establish the mood of the garden. To soften and scent your steps, plant several sturdy herbs that tolerate dry conditions, such as thyme, sage, bergamot, or chamomile, along the course of the path.

You may also choose to line the path with plants that will perfume the air when you brush past them, or whose fragrance tempts you to pause and enjoy the garden's tranquility. Lavender is a powerful stress-reliever, while the rich scents of roses and stocks suggest joyous luxury and indulgence.

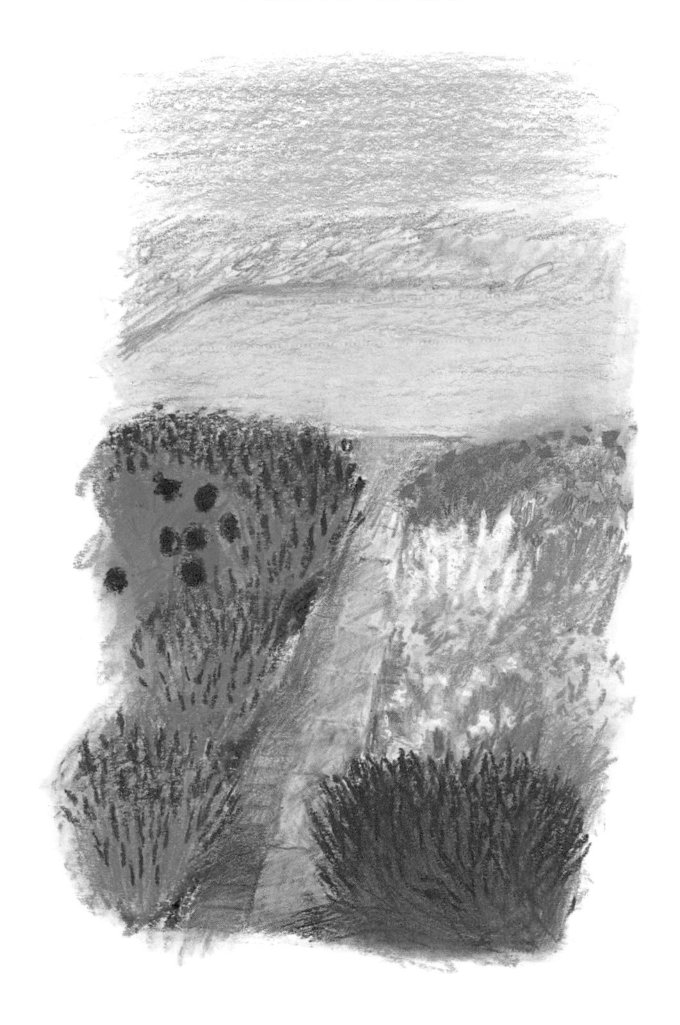

A View for All Seasons

A garden or paved area can look barren and plain at the leanest times of year, but careful plant selection and a little wizardry with pots and other containers can keep the view permanently attractive. Containers create a versatile garden, even in small spaces, allowing shrubs to be moved forward as their buds change to blooms, and then returned to the background when their foliage alone is the main display. Evening-scented flowers can remain in a shady corner during the day, but can be brought to the edge of a doorway or placed by a table when their fragrance is at its height.

- Mix fruits, vegetables, flowers, and herbs for a visually pleasing and fragrant garden. Ornamental cabbages, flowering onions, artichokes and trailing strawberries can all be grown in containers and dotted among more traditional plants.
- If part of the garden becomes flowerless, place a few pots of budding blooms among the foliage to add color to a dull aspect.

The Garden Scene

Color, pattern, and shape can help to create a soothing environment just as effectively outside the home as within it. When planning your garden, try to envision views that will please the eye from a distance and from various angles. Decorate areas of your garden with color-themed beds, featuring either one or a harmonious range of colors. You may choose to integrate different foliage shapes and textures, or to highlight a single large plant within a formal layout. Traditional herbal knot gardens provide enchanting patterns, while box hedging defines the crisp outline of geometric flowerbeds.

Decorative sculpture, ranging from simple urns to life-size figures, provides an imaginative focal point and adds interest to the garden in winter. Privet, yew, and low-growing box can be clipped into charming topiary shapes to provide a further design element.

- "Age" new statuary by brushing it with a film of plain yogurt to encourage the growth of lichen and moss.

• Create simple topiary shapes around chicken wire frames. Wear stout gloves when shaping the wire, then secure the shape in a container or flowerbed and wind the plant shoots around the lower part of the frame. When the frame is well-covered with foliage, trim the shape neatly.

Details of Design

When planning the layout of your garden or patio, consider the diversity of a tranquil countryside scene. Even a small garden contains different habitats within it (such as deep or partial shade, and dry, stony, moist, or water-retaining soil), which can be exploited to include a wide variety of plant life. Carefully positioned grasses, bushes, and trees can provide patterns of light and shade. Strengthen the illusion of a natural landscape by varying plant height, shape, textures, and colors, to bring dramatic interest not only at eye level, but also when sitting in a chair or lounging in a hammock.

To draw attention upward, create a tiered planting scheme by hanging pots on a wall or trellis and filling them with trailing and cascading plants, such as begonias and lobelia. Pots and other containers also allow you to introduce trees and plants that have architectural interest into a garden where space is limited. To give flowerbeds an illusion of depth, place taller shrubs and plants to the back and set lower blooms in front. Fill in around the base with small, colorful plants, for example impatiens or primulas.

Plantings to Soothe and Inspire

Certain plants have a particular beauty or scent that makes them ideal for a peaceful or inspirational garden, especially when their features can be enjoyed all year round. For example, aromatic evergreen trees and shrubs, such as pine, eucalyptus, and rosemary, bring pleasure to several senses throughout the seasons. Decorative screening plants, such as golden hops or the magnificent Virginia creeper, quickly disguise awkward or overbearing structures and create a feeling of privacy and security in the garden area.

Other plants may have a powerful impact over a shorter season. Plan your garden to include some of your favorites for color, shape, and fragrance, then select companions to complement them with year-round interest. Beds of a single color, such as serene white, or a soothing mixture of blues and violets can be very relaxing, especially in a balanced planting that combines elegant spires and trumpet shapes with rounded, starry, and gem-like flowers. A restful garden may also contain plants with tactile qualities that bring you into direct contact with the calming balm of nature—feathery ferns, subtly ribbed hostas, or spectacular, weighty blooms to cradle in your hands.

• Plant bamboo to act as a screen, and enjoy the movement and sounds of its supple fronds swaying majestically in the breeze.

• Underplant trees and shrubs with bright snowdrops, lily-of-the-valley, violets, and bluebonnets, to bring a show of color and scent to leafless or shaded areas of the garden in winter and early spring.

Arbors of Seclusion

The garden offers a perfect location to unwind in an atmosphere of tranquil contemplation. To create the ideal setting for your individual haven, choose a peaceful place—a quiet corner of the lawn or a specially built arch—preferably well away from the noise and activity inside the house. If the outlook contains jarring notes, conceal them with tall or climbing shrubs, or divert the eye with harmonious groupings of flowers or foliage, or an attractive piece of sculpture. You will also need a comfortable seat, perhaps a permanent stone or wooden bench, softened with pillows or rugs, or a canvas garden chair placed in the shade of an overhanging tree.

Spending time in your arbor will bring you close to the pulse of the garden. Here, the gentle hum of bees and dancing of butterflies gradually soothes anxious thoughts, and all your senses, especially smell, are sharpened in the open air. Create your arbor beneath an aromatic pine or cypress tree, or surround it with fragrant plants, such as bushy clumps of lavender, sweet-scented herbs grown in containers, or a trellis laden with roses.

Shade and Structures

A garden or patio that is in bright sunlight in the morning may be in deep shadow by the afternoon—or vice versa. Turn the daily fluctuations of light and shade to your advantage by the clever use of plants, garden furniture, and color. Dull areas can be brightened with a wash of pale paint on the wall or fence—avoid using plain white paint on walls that will reflect sunlight, however, as this may cause glare. At ground level, pale gravel or pebbles and vivid green foliage help to transform a dark corner into a calm retreat.

Trees and tall shrubs—either grown in containers or climbing up trellis-work—bring restful shade to a terrace or roof garden exposed to direct sunlight. Such plants sustain the full impact of the sun, so it is important that they are kept well watered during hot periods.

- A large canvas parasol or awning is a versatile way to provide and direct shade on a balcony or roof garden.
- Tall but light, pampas or bamboo plants grown in containers can be moved around a garden to filter the sun's rays where required.

Trelliswork

Climbing plants grow toward light, spreading over walls and other structures with relentless energy. Given the frame of a latticework arch or pergola, they can be trained into majestic forms to create an intimate space or quiet arbor. Your choice of climbers has an important part to play in defining the mood of your garden haven, since it can address any or all of the principles of shape, light and shade, pattern, texture, color, and fragrance.

A trellis festooned with leaves and flowers effectively adjusts the shape of your garden by adding height, softening hard angles, or screening off less attractive areas. Vines and ivies provide shade and camouflage, and their leaves display an immense variety of shapes, patterns, and textures throughout the year. Flowering climbers add vivid splashes of color: choose species of honeysuckle, rose, or clematis that have a long flowering season. The starry blooms of jasmine or the golden racemes of laburnum even seem to bring their own light into your arbor. A trelliswork structure covered with climbing plants is a perfect place to relax, surrounded by the evocative scents of country-fresh honeysuckle, delicate sweet peas, or luxurious roses.

Moods of the Garden

Throughout the day, magical moments occur that have the power to relax the mind and refresh the spirit. Each of these times has a very individual atmosphere, with colors and sounds that evoke peaceful memories and instill feelings of harmony with nature. A stroll in your garden or a walk in a park allows you to appreciate fully the tranquility of different times of day.

Early morning is a particularly beautiful and quiet time, full of hope and promise. The air is crisp and sweet, dew glistens on leaves as yet unfurled, and rays of light caress the horizon. At first, colors are misty and muted, but as the sun rises the sky is filled with vivid hues of peach, pink, and yellow in a warming canopy of color. As the stillness of the night gives way to bird-song, you can indulge in a pleasant sense of solitude, combined with optimism for the new day. Position a seat in the garden to make the most of the morning light, where you can relax with your tea or coffee, read a newspaper, or meditate in comfort. Enjoy the early calm while you can—all too quickly the tumult and acceleration of the day begin.

Sensual Sunlight

Midday, when the sun is at its zenith, is a time of repose. In hot climates, noon is when shutters are closed and siestas taken—under the shade of a tree, in a hammock, or on a daybed indoors. Inhabitants of colder countries seize the opportunity to bask in the sun's warmth.

Time often seems suspended from ordinary progress. Shimmering heat haze creates a feeling of enchantment, the air is heavy with the scents of blossoms and herbs, and the stillness is interrupted only by the buzz of insects. The contrast between areas of sunlight and shade is at its strongest, and colors are intensified against the dazzling azure of the sky. The poet Walt Whitman captures the mood of sensuous languor: "Give me the splendid silent sun with all his beams full-dazzling...Give me a field where the unmowed grass grows, / Give me an arbor, give me the trellised grape."

- Allow yourself an hour or two to relax completely with a book, or a sketchbook and pencil, away from everyday distractions.

Twilight Hours

Sunset, when the light fades and the evening stars appear, is a peaceful, magical time of day. The progress toward dusk is gradual, bringing subtle change to even a familiar view as light filters slowly from the sky, and gold gives way to soothing deep blues. Dusk is a time of transition between the activity of the day and the stillness of the night. Sounds, such as rustling leaves or the late calls of roosting birds, carry further than in the day, and fragrances also become more intense—stocks, lilies, jasmine, and other evening-scented flowers suffuse the air. White stands out against twilight's muted colors, so feature it—as blooms or garden furniture—in and around your evening arbor. Sensuous summer heat also lingers: enjoy the last of the day's warmth in quiet reflection or relaxation with family and friends.

- Keep flying insects at bay and scent your arbor, patio, or porch with the lemony aroma of citronella candles.
- As light diminishes, place garden candles against a mirror to echo the sparkling of the evening stars.

Mysterious Moonlight

When the dark blanket of night falls across the sky, nature's color palette is reduced and simplified, and the garden is transformed by the silvery light of the moon. The silence is occasionally broken by the sounds of nocturnal animals gathering food or the hooting of an owl, but otherwise this is a quiet time, when the mind and body can unwind in preparation for sleep.

The moon itself may be perceived as a watchful presence—"the man in the moon"—or as the focus for mystery and magic: its cycle is often believed to influence human emotion. Moonlight strikes a glimmering path across a pond and highlights the foam on the crest of a wave. Echo these effects with garden lighting positioned near a water feature such as a pool or fountain. Other artificial lighting can be varied to suit your mood. Beams directed through the branches of a tree give it a magical, almost surreal quality; brightly-colored Japanese lanterns create a relaxed atmosphere.

- Simple, elegant strings of bulbs can be woven randomly through bushes or arranged more formally on garden structures.

Features of Serenity

To achieve a tranquil environment we need not always consider the grand scale—in fact, this may be impracticable in a shared apartment or workplace. Instead, we can look to small refinements that define our own personal quiet place. To some, water is an enchanting source of serenity; others may find that their spirits are refreshed by the sound of birdsong or the contemplation of a flower or a treasured photograph. Troubled thoughts may be stilled by a look back in time or the simple elegance of contemporary design. The secret is to find your own key to the realm of serenity.

Soothing Waters

The presence of water brings us into harmony with the natural world. To regain a sense of tranquility, we have only to listen to the sound of rain on leaves, gaze at a calm pond, or enjoy the enveloping embrace of water by floating in a swimming pool or lying in a deep bath. In the office or when traveling, refresh your face with a mineral water spray, or cool your wrists with eau de cologne. The restorative power of water is widely acknowledged, and certain beliefs invest rivers and lakes with magical qualities.

Any garden can feature water, from a pool or lake to a large tub. The concentric circles or gentle ripples that appear when the surface is disturbed—by wind, a fish, or a falling leaf—have a mesmerizing and soothing effect. Surround your water garden with tall, water-loving plants, such as irises and reeds, to add color, life, and an air of seclusion.

- Water lilies need an open, sunny location, but not necessarily a vast area of water: miniature types have flowers only two inches across.

Flowing Water

The sounds and sensation of flowing water always refresh, bringing life, movement, and a softly babbling "voice" to any setting. Whether natural or artificial, waterfalls and fountains introduce a note of vitality that can revive weary spirits. We need only to listen and watch as the water dances and catches the light. Larger homes and offices may incorporate flowing water in an interior or pool area, perhaps falling from a spout or in a steady, sheet-like cascade. A garden can feature a simple jet of water running over a bed of rounded rocks or down regular steps of chiseled stone. More formal variations may include a landscaped waterfall or elegant fountain.

- Try a Japanese bamboo flowform, which directs water around a small circuit—the rhythmic sound of the bamboo pipes as they continually empty and refill with water is extremely soothing.
- Buy a desktop "wave maker"—thick, colored liquid encased in clear plastic. Tilt it gently to set it in motion, then silence the buzz of troubled thoughts by focusing on its rhythmic ebb and flow.

Water and Stillness

The many settings and moods of water—from stormy seas to quiet ponds—echo human emotions. In your home and workplace, use water as a point of reference on which to focus and still your mind. For example, a tank of fish is relaxing to watch and can give a few moments' respite from the hustle and bustle of everyday life. You can also create a simple indoor water feature by covering the base of a large glass vase or bowl with colored marbles or pebbles and filling the vessel with water; double its effect of serenity by placing the bowl against a mirror. As the water is disturbed by air currents it will swirl or ripple with a gentle, fluid motion. Highlight the soothing movement of the water by placing flower heads or floating candles on the surface. The colors of the flowers or candles can be varied to suit your mood.

• Apartment dwellers without a garden can grow avocado stones, or hyacinth and similar bulbs in water alone. "Plant" them in glass containers with just the base of the stone or bulb touching the water, and watch their roots and shoots gradually appear.

• Create a tranquil table setting by giving each diner a finger bowl filled with water and strewn with flower petals or thin slices of lemon.

• Make an attractive stress-buster by filling a decorative glass bottle with water—perhaps tinting it pale green or blue—then adding coarse sand and sealing the bottle well. When troubled thoughts threaten to overwhelm you, shake the bottle, then replace it on your desk. Watch the sand as it slowly settles and calm returns.

Sound and Motion

Even in the tranquility of your quiet place, silence may sometimes be insufficient to still recurring worries or anxious thoughts. To reach a deeper level of relaxation, reflect upon the sounds of the natural world, often essentially linked with movement: the ebb and flow of the sea, the whisper of wind in a cornfield, the gentle sprinkling of summer rain, and the wintry cawing of crows returning home at dusk. The serenity of an indoor haven is closely linked to an awareness of nature's patterns; relaxation tapes often feature such sounds to calm and refresh, and the soothing play of wind chimes offers an enchanting bridge between indoor and outdoor worlds.

- Create your own forms of wind chimes, for example using shells or pieces of rounded and opaque glass washed ashore by the sea. Lengths of wide bamboo also make a pleasant, hollow sound.
- Make a bird ball of nuts and seeds and hang it outside your window to bring the pleasure of bird plumage and song into your day.

Rhythms of Rest

Rhythmic swaying, musical beats, or repetitious motion can create a mood of sensuous relaxation that is almost hypnotic. The regular swing of a grandfather clock's pendulum or a Newton's cradle on an office desk encourages concentration and calm, contemplative thought. Poetry is often written to a rhythm, and reciting or listening to some favorite lines is also very soothing.

The repetition of a sound or action time after time, such as a heartbeat or the fall of waves on the shore, creates feelings of reassurance and serenity. Predictable rhythms of sound and movement are strangely comforting; a cat purring in your lap or the deep breathing of someone sleeping provide a calm background against which the day's anxieties fade away. Rhythm is the basis of meditation techniques, quietly stilling the mind's stresses; it is also soporific, as parents instinctively realize when they rock a child to sleep.

• Create a mobile from natural materials: flower petals, sprays of leaves or berries, seed heads, feathers, small pine cones, and nuts. Tie these with thread onto a slim tree branch or coat hanger, and position

it over a radiator. The rising currents of warm air will make the lighter objects twist and turn as if they were floating on the breeze.

• If you have difficulty getting to sleep, place a softly ticking clock beside your bed. To help you to relax, concentrate on the rhythms of your breathing and let them harmonize with the sound of the clock.

Stirrings of Foliage

Among the most evocative of natural sounds is that of wind in the trees, whether it is the gentle rustle of a summer breeze or the bluster of a gale in the fall, when the protective aspect of your private haven can be fully savored. Even in a small garden, trees have distinctive voices, from the whisper of the willow's fronds to the murmur of pine trees and the majestic sighing of the oak. Gentler gusts ripple the foliage of wall climbers, such as Virginia creeper, ivies, and vines, heralding the decline of summer. These calming sounds can be remembered indoors through a variety of decorative designs and mementoes.

- Bring branches of leaves into the house and display them in a vase, both when fresh, with cut blossom or flowers, and after drying. The dried leaves make a colorful indoor arrangement for the winter or fall.
- Glue dried leaves and grasses to the outside of a plain, pale-colored lampshade and add a coat of varnish to preserve them. Their shapes will cast a delightful shadow pattern on the surrounding walls.

• Press gloriously colored leaves and either frame them singly, as a series of small pictures, or arrange them together in one large frame.

• Using a dried, pressed leaf as a stencil, paint a seasonal frieze on your windows with a water-soluble paint.

Echoes of Time

There are many design classics, pieces of furniture and equipment that may have been superseded by technology but whose pleasing shape, history, and charm cannot be outdone by modern fashion. Having withstood the test of time, these items bring a sense of peaceful continuity to even the most contemporary apartment setting.

Well-designed pieces—for example, a sturdy chair, a solid dining table, a comfortable sofa, or smaller items such as kitchen equipment or garden tools—remain attractive and functional, and updated copies are now in production. An object need not be genuinely old to have enduring appeal. Choose classics to establish your own mood of peace: they may have personal associations, such as a Bakelite telephone like one you remember from your grandfather's office, or a bentwood chair similar to that in your mother's bedroom; or they may fulfill a long-held desire to own, say, a chrome toaster or electric fan.

Memories

Within any home there are sure to be reminders of the past, whether recent or long ago. These reminders come in many guises, from photographs, souvenirs or a child's painting, to a cup and saucer from a grandmother's tea service. Such items are seldom of great monetary value but are priceless and irreplaceable to their owners.

Mementoes may trigger periods of reverie, when one can draw strength and spiritual refreshment from images of the past. Objects found on a recent country walk—leaves, flowers, nuts, or pebbles—will help you to remember a peaceful day. A photograph taken on a special vacation or at a family occasion can quiet troubled thoughts by evoking pleasant memories.

With their links to times gone by, such items are friendly and reassuring. They can go a long way toward personalizing office space, or, when arranged in a new house or apartment, they can be the first stage in turning it into a home. A single object may complement a room's overall decoration or become a focal point in its own right, while a group of these precious pieces and photographs can form the basis for a treasure table or shelf.

Period Features

An heirloom, an old piece of furniture, or delicate china that has been given as a gift or found in an antique shop may have a special appeal, not only because it is a treasure in its own right, but also because it reflects a period or style for which you feel an affinity. Just one item can be the starting point for a collection of similar objects from that era and, in some cases, can inspire a room to be decorated and furnished to invoke the atmosphere of that time. Perhaps an existing feature within your home, such as exposed beams, a wood-paneled ceiling, a Victorian hearth, or Art Deco tiles, suggests a collection of complementary items. A pleasing effect can also be achieved by combining pieces from various eras, linking them through color and form instead of period.

Old objects bring a nostalgic ambience to any room, with the warmth and mellowness that come with age. Often, they will have been handmade—sewn, embroidered, painted, or carved—with love, care, and skill. Each handmade item is unique; there never has been and never will be another piece exactly the same.

• Set a single antique or piece of furniture against a plain background. Let it free the imagination by drawing you into its own time and space.

• Give new lace and cotton an aged look by dipping them in diluted coffee or tea. This will soften the whiteness of modern materials.

Still Lifes

The creative arrangement of objects can introduce a note of order and serenity to any room in your home. Simple, everyday items, such as glasses, flowers, fruit, or shells, often make the most effective still lifes, the impact of which lies less in their individual components than in the overall display. Composing still lifes is a very personal art; choose harmonious colors and shapes that will relate well to one another and to the space around them. Small ornaments on a shelf, for example, may be most successfully placed in small, odd numbered groups rather than in a continuous, evenly spaced line.

The diverse colors and scents of flowers can bring an imaginative focus to still-life groupings. Ikebana, the Japanese art of flower arranging, emphasizes form and balance in its deceptively simple compositions. A single spray or individual bloom may be placed upright in a plain container, the shape and texture of its petals enhanced by a single green leaf or a piece of twisted wood. Traditionally, the flower head itself is slightly angled, because it is held to be "impolite" for the flower to stare directly at the observer.

Nature's Bounty

Many of the most attractive still-life features can be found in the varied treasure of the natural world. In composing an arrangement of fruit and flowers, nuts and seeds, pieces of bark, and glistening feathers, it is often tempting to include too overwhelming an assortment: an excess of items may diminish the final result. A simple, plain-colored, or terracotta dish offers a harmonious background for one perfect, delicate pear, a clutch of gleaming apples, or the sensuous, velvety texture of blue-black grapes. Even in a more complex grouping, the beauty of nature's produce deserves individual attention. Juxtapose the gentle curves of uncut fruit with segments of dried peel and pips, and offset a cluster of rounded, rich orange gourds with the spiky seed heads of poppy or teasel.

Natural still lifes can easily accommodate a seasonal theme, reflecting the changing year in their selection of fresh or dried fruit, nuts and pine cones, petals and bulbs. Potpourri may contribute interesting shapes as well as fragrance, and natural materials, such as wicker, hessian, linen, or cotton complement and frame the arrangement.

• To preserve fresh flowers, hang a bunch of cut flowers upside down in a dry, well-ventilated room.

• Make attractive decorations from apple rings. Core and slice the apples into medium rings and steep in salted water for ten minutes. Thread the rings on a stick and allow to dry for two or three days.

Seashore Harvest

Some of the most inspirational touches in a home cannot be bought from a designer store but are rich in memories and personal significance. A truly individual collection might include shells from an empty beach, coral or a fossil found on a family vacation, or a piece of driftwood picked up and carried home. Such things have importance beyond any material value and may become a focus for periods of serene reflection.

To show the elements of a seashore still life to best advantage, take care to group them in a compatible way. Large objects are best kept to the back, those of medium size in the middle, and the smallest items at the front. Such an arrangement will create an imaginative illusion of depth and perspective. Think carefully about the colors and textures of each object: strong and dark colors should be kept to the back, with lighter and translucent items at the front. Juxtapose rough and smooth surfaces for interest—for example, spiky, intricate coral will complement a gently rounded pebble.

• Dry shells and pebbles may appear pale and powdery; place them in a glass bowl or vase filled with water and see their colors become rich and vibrant and their patterns come alive.

• Rather than decide which view of a shell or other found object is most attractive, place pieces on a glass shelf, or next to a mirror, to enjoy them from all angles.

• Revive seaside memories by holding a convoluted seashell to your ear. The internal spiral reproduces the soothing, rhythmic sound of waves falling on the shore.

• A collection of seashells or driftwood can also be used to frame a bathroom mirror. Glue the shells directly to the wall around the glass, or make a separate frame into which the mirror can be set.

Living in Tranquility

The peace and security of our individual havens may seem far removed from the innumerable pressures of everyday life. Yet quiet places are more than a particular location, albeit one with the power to refresh and revitalize. They represent a state of mind, an inner strength and calm that, with practice, we can draw upon at will. By learning to visualize a beloved setting, recapture the scent of a favorite flower, or remember a happy moment, we can restore balance and perspective to difficult and stressful situations. True havens exist in the heart and imagination as well as in our homes and gardens, and they will offer us a private sanctuary as long as we dwell in them.

Index

INDEX

Acknowledgments

The publishers wish to thank the following photographers and organizations for their permission to reproduce the photographs in this book.

1 Robert Harding Syndication/Polly Wreford/*Homes and Gardens*/©IPC Magazines; 9 Michael Freeman; 10 Elizabeth Whiting & Associates/Jean-Paul Bonhommet; 14 Robert Harding Syndication/Nadia MacKenzie/*Country Homes & Interiors*/©IPC Magazines; 17 Elizabeth Whiting & Associates/ Rodney Hyett; 19 David Phelps; 21 Arcaid/Alan Weintraub/by courtesy of Molly and Donn Chappellet; 23 Paul Ryan/*International Interiors*/Laura Bohn; 27 David Phelps; 35 Michael Freeman; 37 Robert Harding Syndication/Paul Ryan/*Homes & Gardens*/ ©IPC Magazines; 39 Elizabeth Whiting & Associates/Mark Luscombe-Whyte/designer Christina Fallah; 41 Elizabeth Whiting & Associates/ Dennis Stone/designer Dave Bollon; 43 The Interior Archive/Simon Upton; 45 Elizabeth Whiting & Associates; 47 Robert Harding Syndication/James Merrell/*Options*/©IPC Magazines; 49 Jan Baldwin/Kate Otten, Johannesburg, South Africa; 51 Christian Sarramon; 53 Robert Harding Syndication/Fritz von der Schulenburg/*Country Homes & Interiors*/©IPC Magazines; 57 Robert Harding Syndication/ Tom Leighton/*Homes & Gardens*/©IPC Magazines; 59 The Interior Archive/Fritz von der Schulenburg; 61 Christian Sarramon; 64 Jan Baldwin; 65 Robert Harding Syndication/Andreas von Einsiedel/*Homes & Gardens*/©IPC Magazines; 66 Christian Sarramon; 71 Robert Harding Syndication/Tom Leighton/ *Homes & Gardens*/©IPC Magazines; 73 S&O Mathews; 75 and 77 The Interior Archive/Fritz von der Schulenburg; 81 Michael Freeman; 83 The Interior Archive/ Fritz von der Schulenburg; 85 Jan Baldwin; 87 Elizabeth Whiting & Associates/Nadia MacKenzie; 91 Paul Ryan/ *International Interiors*/ Sasha Waddell; 95 Jan Baldwin/Roger Oates, Herefordshire, England; 98 Christian Sarramon; 101 Paul Ryan/*International Interiors*/Marcel Wolterinck; 105 Elizabeth Whiting & Associates/Neil Lorimer; 109 Andrew Lawson/Gothic House, Oxfordshire; 111 Jerry Harpur/designer Bruce Kelly, New York; 113 Robert Harding Picture Library/ Andreas von Einsiedel/ *Country Homes & Interiors*/ ©IPC Magazines; 115 Clive Nichols/designer Arabella Lennox-Boyd; 117 Jerry Harpur/designer Kristin Fenderson, New Hampshire; 119 Jerry Harpur/Ingeborg Hecht, New York City; 123 Jerry Harpur/"Dolwen", Llanrhaeadr-ym-Monchnant, Powys, Wales; 125 Jerry Harpur/designer Edwina von Gal; 127 Jerry Harpur/designer Phillip Watson, Fredericksburg, Virginia; 129 Jerry Harpur/ designer Victor Nelson, New York City; 130 Robert Harding Syndication/Bill Reavell/*Homes & Ideas*/ ©IPC Magazines; 135 Michael Freeman; 141 Elizabeth Whiting & Associates/Spike Powell; 145 Arcaid/Simon Kenny/*Belle*; 147 Jan Baldwin/Sid & Cathy Benson, Langebaan, South Africa; 149 Elizabeth Whiting & Associates/ Rodney Hyett; 153 Elizabeth Whiting & Associates/Rodney Hyett; 157 The Interior Archive/Andrew Wood.